EM

Empath for Beginners – Empath Survival Guide to Understanding your Emotions, Energy, and Gift

[JASON BENNETT]

Legal & Disclaimer

The information contained in this book and its contents is not designed to replace or take the place of any form of medical or professional advice; and is not meant to replace the need for independent medical, financial, legal or other professional advice or services, as may be required. The content and information in this book has been provided for educational and entertainment purposes only.

The content and information contained in this book has been compiled from sources deemed reliable, and it is accurate to the best of the Author's knowledge, information and belief. However, the Author cannot guarantee its accuracy and validity and cannot be held liable for any errors and/or omissions. Further, changes are periodically made to this book as and when needed. Where appropriate and/or necessary, you must consult a professional (including but not limited to your doctor, attorney, financial advisor or such

Table of Contents

Empaths – Who They Are and Knowing If You Are One

Tell me something. How does the word Empath sound to you? EMPATH... Say it in your head. Isolate it from every other thought and *really* say it. Feel every single syllable. Feel each sound that the word makes from start to finish, and think about how it really feels to you.

Does it speak to you? Can you feel it say something, hint at something? Do you feel like there's a very deep, underlying current to the word that goes beyond the everyday understanding of things, the mundane existence of life on this planet? Does the word tug at something inside you that you can feel but it isn't physical; like it's in your mind, and is pulling you?

Are you totally feeling weird, lost, and confused right now and thinking I've gone stark raving mad, or are you nodding your head in agreement to at least some of the above questions? If you are one of the head nodders, then you very well may be an empath.

Empaths have been around from the beginning of time. The word 'empath' is very similar to empathy, which goes beyond just feeling bad for another person, which is sympathy. It means actually being able to put oneself in another person's shoes and experiencing their feelings. Sympathy, on the contrary, leans more towards pity. The person feels bad for another, but not much else. Sympathy often doesn't invoke compassion or lead to any constructive help. Empathetic people have the ability to understand what the other person is going through or has been through, and hence have more compassion and the will to help.

Empathic people go a step further. They have the ability to literally feel the emotions of other people. It is difficult for those around the really understand an empath. Empaths are very open and expressive people that can often be termed as weird. They are the ones with the eclectic friend circle, who often keep to themselves, and come across as loners or para-social people.

The main question, though, is whether you are an empath, and secondly, whether you know that you are. Empaths display very particular traits that set them apart from others. These qualities cannot be found in a non-empath and is hence difficult for them to understand why empaths think and act in a certain way.

Traits of empaths – Know if you are one

Just knowing things

How many times has it happened that someone asked you any of these following questions or something along the same lines?

"How on earth did you know that?" or

"How do you always know what to say to make me feel better?" or

"I had never thought of that, how do you always come up with such insightful stuff?" or

"How do you manage to get so deep into the psychology of everyday things? We didn't even realize that!" (Okay, that was slightly too specific)

And the age-old gem, "Why do you think so much?"

One of the primary traits of empaths is that they 'just know' stuff. Information. For example, they have the ability to understand how someone is feeling, can find solutions to perplexing problems, or possess general insights about life that other people do not think of. This empathic trait often surpasses the information caught by even the keenest and observant of eyes, and goes much deeper than what it appears to be. Empaths are generally unaware of how they know a particular piece of information, or where it came from. It is a 'knowing' that goes deeper than a gut feeling or intuition. To an empath, this seems like the information has just come to them when they needed it, as a means to move forward in a difficult situation. Like a solution or a guiding light.

Feeling other people's emotions

Empaths can actually pick up on the emotions of the people around them and feel them as their own. This is a very common trait in empaths, and can cause a lot of confusion if you are new at it, especially since you don't know where so many emotions are coming from. It is difficult for empaths to differentiate between their feelings and those of others, at times. It is also often a struggle for them to focus on being in the moment and concentrating on the 'now' because of the plethora of emotions surrounding them.

Empaths who are more control of their ability and know how to use it well can even sense when someone is not being true to them or when someone is thinking unpleasant or negative thoughts about them. They can see through the facades that people put up and the falsity that people display. Many times, empaths do not even need to be in close physical proximity of a person to feel their emotions. Some can feel the emotions of those who are far away if there is a strong emotional bond between them.

Needing a lot of alone time after public events

As you know, one of the primary traits of an empath is picking up and absorbing the emotions of other people. So, understandably, they are not very fond of public places and events like concerts, weddings, parties, crowded clubs, holiday outings at popular hangouts that attract huge crowds, or even something as mundane as going to the market on a weekend. There are so many emotions of varying intensities and types in the air that dealing with them all can become a real challenge for an empath. Their own emotions are thrown around in various directions, making it rather chaotic and noisy for them. Imagine feeling happy and sad and gleeful and excited and angry and frustrated continuously one after the other, and sometimes simultaneously.

If an empath has had to attend a lot of public events in a short span of time or a major event with a lot of people, then they need some downtime to cool off and regain their emotional energy. Being surrounded by hordes of people emanating various emotions is severely exhausting for an empath as it can send their system into overdrive. To prevent themselves from experiencing a burnout, empaths take breaks from the outside world, sometimes for days at a time, to recuperate and recharge.

Always being drawn towards the helpless/troubled

Empaths are always naturally drawn to those in need. They gravitate towards animals and people who are in a helpless position, down, depressed, oppressed, bullied, or just in need of some comfort. Empaths never discriminate among any living beings. To them, everyone is equal. They can feel the energies those around them and pick up their emotions. Empaths can also see through those who are appear 'happy' and 'okay', but are hiding their true pain and suffering behind this false exterior. They naturally understand when someone needs a listening ear or sounding board. Hence, they are often able to help people in denial to open up about their feelings and unburden themselves, and even get professional help if needed. It is quite difficult to lie to an empath by saying that everything is okay because more often than not, they see right through it. This ability to feel compassion and care enough to indulge is very rare and not found very often in the outside world.

Intolerance towards violence and cruelty

Empaths are inherently loving and caring people because they have the gift of knowing and understanding the innermost emotions of other beings. Reading about or watching news involving violence or cruelty towards other people or animals can make them very uncomfortable and depressed, to the point where they may even stop reading or watching the news. Even otherwise, empaths are very much against cruelty to animals, nature, and humans. Many empaths are vegetarians because they can feel the emotions and pain of the animal, especially knowing if it suffered. Some claim to feel the remnant energies of the animal on their plate, which deters them from eating meat. Drama, pessimism, and intense negative emotions bother them greatly, and it is very difficult for them to comprehend how people can be so cruel.

Become a natural sounding board for people

Empaths are natural listeners, which is why they tend to take up the roles of healers and helpers. They have a healing, positive energy that calls out to people who need to talk and offload or are looking for some kind of help. Empaths often find themselves listening and offering comfort to people who come and start talking to them about their lives, problems, woes, everything, out of the blue. Many times, these people don't intend to share all their thoughts and feelings, but it's the warm and welcoming energy of an empath that tugs at them. However, given the nature of empaths to take on other people's emotions, it is important to be careful so as not to make the problems of others into their own and get too involved.

Intense relationships

Empaths tend to have intense love affairs and friendships. Because they are so perceptive and intuitive, they love to get into the minds of people that they like. Romantic relationships with empaths tend to get very deep and intense at a very fast pace. Taking it nice and slow doesn't really fit into the empath psyche. They just can't help it. Empaths connect on a deep and profound level very quickly and get thoroughly involved in their partner's emotions and energy, blending it with their own. Even in friendships, empaths tend to connect on a level that usually takes years, in a short span of time. They don't have difficulty understanding people, and hence, all their relationships are deep and intimate and develop very quickly.

Empaths also tend to blame less and defend more, even if other people hurt them. Because they have a deeper understanding of people's behavior, they often give reasons and sometimes even make excuses for why others act in a certain way. This can sometimes be harmful to empaths because they ignore their own benefit for that of others, which can be taken advantage of. Empaths are also prone to addictions to alcohol, sex, drugs, shopping, etc. This is their defense mechanism or form of self-preservation to block out the external energies that they are attracting and absorbing.

Always being intensely curious about life and the universe

Empaths are the most curious of creatures, always asking questions and trying to find answers. They are not satisfied with answers that just skim the surface, and love to dig deeper. Empaths often possess a curiosity and questions that can stump other people because they go beyond the mundane and shallow. Empaths always look for a deeper meaning within things, like a spoken or written word, expression, tone, or situations. They love analyzing situations and understanding them on a deeper level. Their questions are along the lines of life, philosophy, and the universe, but don't just leave it at that. They try and find the answers.

Going beyond face value

When an empath is in the midst of a conversation, they don't just hear and respond. It isn't enough to tell an empath something and hope that they will just accept it. Empaths analyze the other person's words, tone, volume, changes in pitch, and body language. They will try to catch the meaning behind your words to understand the hidden intention, like falsity, sarcasm, anger, teasing, or naughtiness. Reading between the lines is their thing. Hence, it is easier for empaths to catch when they are being lied to, when someone is being phony, or when the intentions coming their way are harmful. However, empaths who haven't harnessed their gift yet should be careful of such people because of their selfless nature of putting others before themselves.

Experience unexplained physical issues

Empaths often experience aches and pains that are quite inexplicable. Just like emotions, they also pick up on the physical discomfort of other people. Hence, they can develop the same or similar symptoms, or else some other form of physical unease. A novice empath will not be able to explain this sudden feeling of discomfort. Empaths commonly suffer from lower back pain and digestive problems. The solar plexus chakra, which is the emotional center of the body, is located in the stomach area. Empaths absorb the emotional energies of other people, and an overload of these energies can affect the chakra and weaken it. Hence, empaths can face a range of tummy issues ranging from small to severe.

Another thing that you'll agree with if you're an empath is the constant fatigue. Empaths are 'tired' most of the time. And it's not from doing too much physical activity. A lot of incoming emotional energy can cause an empath to be emotionally drained. And if they don't get that their necessary dose of alone time, then the symptoms start showing in the form of physical fatigue. You may often hear an empath say that they are 'emotionally tired'. It means that they have been around too many people lately without a break.

Often found in care giving or creative professions

Empaths are naturally drawn towards professions that involve volunteer work, caring for other living beings, and those that allow an outlet for their creativity. Many empaths choose careers such as veterinary, nursing, medicine, teaching, occupational therapy, counseling, environmental studies, and volunteering. These people are also natural dancers, writers, singers, painters, musicians, and tend to cultivate their natural talent in many creative fields. Empaths make great storytellers and are inherently curious about their ancestry and history. It isn't surprising to see an empath is possession of a family tree or some family heirlooms, even having many stories and fables about their ancestors. Empaths often go all out when caring for another being, and work without any complaints or expectations. They are very generous and selfless people with a lot of love, care, and compassion to give. Owing to their gift, these people understand the suffering, afflictions, or needs of others better than most.

Can be unpredictable

Empaths can have many moods depending on the people that they are surrounded by. Sometimes, they even pick up on the emotions of others when they are alone. So, it is very natural that their own feelings can change from one moment to the other, which in turn affects their activities. They can swing from happy to miserable in seconds, and lose all interest in doing whatever they were doing just a minute ago.

Empaths tend to enjoy music a lot, but don't stick to one particular genre. The 'mood' of music they want to listen to depends on their own. It may so happen that they are listening to a song and halfway through it, switch to another totally different genre. Lyrics of a song can greatly affect an empath, especially if it is pertinent to something that has happened in the recent past. The empath can get completely lost in the lyrics or feel the intense emotions that it brings out. For example, if the empath is in a good mood and listens to a happy song, he/she can start dancing, giggling, jumping around, etc. And if it's the other way around, then the sad lyrics or music can even bring the empath to tears, kill their appetite, or send them into a depression.

Introverts in nature

Although empaths are very open and expressive people, they are often introverts by nature. This is because is easy for them to always be overwhelmed by the emotions and energies of others around them. Hence, they prefer to limit their interactions to a small group of people, or even better, to one-on-one meet-ups. They do not have large groups of friends, but a smaller group comprising of singular people who don't know each other.

When empaths are with these friends, they are can be very open. It is a unique quality of empaths to be able to talk about things that other people refrain from; for instance, life problems which others might find embarrassing to discuss. Empaths believe that being open and communicating freely is the best way to lighten the soul of its burdens. And because they are already absorbing so much from the outside world, talking about things really helps them.

Intuitive and psychic in nature

Empaths have an inbuilt intuition or 'psychic abilities'. Their gut feeling about the most unexpected things is usually right in the end. Although this is a natural gift, empaths need to hone it and make it stronger. It is not wise for them to trust their gut feeling if they are emotionally involved in something. Their own emotions and energies plus those of others around them can cloud their judgment if they are novices or have no idea of their abilities. An empath who has strong control over their empathic skills can better trust their judgment as it is objective and unattached to any emotions.

Get bored or distracted easily

Empaths are easily bored or distracted. Unless they can find an activity that is not only mentally stimulating but also emotionally fulfilling, they have difficulty maintaining prolonged focus and interest. Unless they can find a teacher that goes beyond the technicalities of a subject and exudes passion, teaching through real examples, their interest in the subject dwindles.

Given that empaths are very prone to daydreaming, it is very easy for them to switch off and go into their own world. These are the people who absolutely cannot do something that they don't like. It feels to them as if they are living a lie, which goes against the basic empath nature. Until they find something that they truly connect with, empaths keep waiting and searching, which very often gives them the 'lazy' tag. Coercing them to do something through guilt or by putting them down will make them extremely unhappy, and absolutely disinterested in doing the work. The situation can spiral out of control and become a really miserable one in no time.

Love nature, Hate clutter

Empaths turn to nature to replenish their soul. They are truly nature people, and love spending time with the birds, trees, and animals. They have a special connection with animals and can understand what they are going through by communicating with them.

Solitude is something that they crave very deeply, and it is literally physically important for them to recharge. Empaths are free spirited, and prefer the outdoors to being inside. These are some of the most minimalist people you will find. They absolutely hate clutter because it blocks their energy and makes it difficult to focus on anything. Their homes or rooms are usually clear, with only the required pieces of furniture and other items. What they don't need, they don't keep.

It isn't just restricted to their physical surroundings, but empaths also dislike clutter in the form of strict rules, too much control, or a mundane routine. It makes them feel smothered and suffocated. Just the prospect of having to let go of their freedom can put an empath on edge, which is why they are often seen in professions that either allow their naturally caring nature to come forward or lets them to work on their own hours.

Excellent Listeners

Empaths are excellent listeners because of their gift. People find themselves naturally drawn towards an empath, and talking about their deepest feelings without even intending to. The feeling of comfort that an empath exudes puts people at ease immediately. They know that this person will not judge them, pay close attention, actually understand what they are going through, and display a lot of empathy, understanding, and offer sound advice. Even though an empath may not necessarily be giving advice, people just feel like they can be themselves and vent around this person. Empaths generally don't talk about themselves unless they are in the company of someone they are extremely comfortable with. They know the level of understanding that they personally need when sharing something and hence tend to be open only around people who can provide them with that understanding.

Can't Stand Narcissists and Emotional Vampires

Narcissistic people are a real pain in the neck for empaths, and they simply cannot stand them. Empaths cannot digest the fact that there are people who can think only about themselves and talk only about themselves and not take other people's feelings into consideration.

Empaths are also a very easy target for emotional vampires. Emotional vampires are those who suck the emotional energy out of other people. These people need constant attention from others and are always looking for someone to dump their emotions on. They like to elicit emotional reactions from people and then feed off of those. Their relationships are never healthy. The main traits of emotional vampires are that they suffer from low self-esteem, need an excessive amount of attention or validation, cannot be emotionally self-sufficient or strong, and always believe that they it is never their fault. Empaths are excellent victims for emotional vampires because of their nature. An empath will listen and empathize with an emotional vampire and go all out to help them. This makes them easy targets.

Mood Swings

What an empath looks like to the world depends greatly on how he/she is feeling. Empaths tend to have mood swings depending on where they are physically and whom they are surrounded by. If they are surrounded by too many people or negative energies, they will appear tired, aloof, reserved, withdrawn, or downright miserable. They have a hard time pretending to put up a happy face if they are feeling low. They are always very open, expressive, and explicit; you can call them open books. It is very easy to catch on that they're not in the best of spirits, though to most people, the reason isn't always very clear. This can lead to empaths being labeled as depressing, moody, and boring, withdrawn, or plain rude. An empath can surprise you with the array of emotions that they display. One moment, they can be totally miserable, and the next, very jolly.

Extreme sensitivity to their environment

Empaths are very sensitive to their surroundings. They can sense what is happening around them even when other people cannot. For instance, empaths can go to some place where a lot of people are present and just 'sense' the mood without anyone having said a word. Funnily enough, empaths can even sense the day of the week. Even if they aren't going to an office or college or school, they can feel the 'Monday blues' and 'Friday excitement'. Many empaths, unbeknownst to themselves, hate activities like flying, sitting in amusement park rides, watching shows that provoke extreme unpleasant emotions.

Cannot be rude to people

Empaths find it inherently impossible to retort to people, even if they have been wronged. Many empaths can be termed as weak or gutless because of their lack of ability to be mean or rude to people. That is far from the truth though.

Most empaths simply cannot be knowingly or purposely hurtful to another being because that is their nature. They absorb the emotions of other people and understand where the other person is coming from. This knowledge prevents them from reacting in the same way to the other person. Empaths who are more in control of their gift are able to form better responses that allow them to stand up for themselves while saving them a lot of guilt.

These are the most common qualities of empathic people. If you agree to most of these, then you are definitely one of them. Remember that even if some traits don't agree with your personality, it doesn't mean that you aren't an empath. Everyone is different, and what matters is the feeling that you get after reading this.

Misconceptions about Empaths

Although empaths possess the ability to absorb the emotional energies and frequencies of others, these gifts are very internal and often times can't be explained by the possessors themselves. Empaths are often misunderstood because of this. Since they cannot understand what is happening to them or convince other people of their abilities without sounding crazy, they stand a greater chance of being labeled as moody, lazy, weird, or selfish. Here are some common misconceptions about empaths and why they are wrong. So, the next time you feel someone is behaving in any of the following ways or someone says the same about you, remember to read this.

Empaths are self-centered

This is actually far from the truth. Empaths are more outward focused than inward. They pick up on the emotional energies of other people and absorb them. They land up mixing their own feelings with these external impulses, which makes them uncomfortable and sometimes confused. This state of emotional being wreaks havoc on an empath's mental state, causing them to retreat into a shell and not interact with people. This behavior is often wrongly perceived as self-centered or self-absorbed. Empaths cannot explain why they feel the way they do, which gives a different impression to an outsider.

Empaths are unstable

Empaths are more responsive to the negative stimuli around them, which throws their mental well-being off balance. Because of their natural magnetism, people gravitate towards empaths to emotionally unload themselves. This emotional baggage puts a lot of pressure on the empath, making it hard for them to easily let go of this negative energy. Empaths can go into a depression or 'down' state of mind if exposed to negative energies for a long time, even suffering from some physical symptoms.

Empaths are lazy or moody

Empaths absolutely detest doing something that they don't like. When we say don't like, it means anything that doesn't give them a sense of emotional and spiritual fulfillment. Coaxing an empath to do things out of guilt or criticism might convince them to do it, but they will be very miserable and depressed. They can take a while to figure out their true calling in life. An empath cannot do things that are false or dishonest as it goes against their nature and makes them very unhappy. All this combined with the mish-mash of energies can be misunderstood as laziness, lack of drive, or moodiness.

Empaths are mentally and emotionally weak

Empaths are highly-sensitive people, but not all sensitive people are empaths. Owing to the hundreds of emotions that they are bombarded with, empaths are prone to be more emotional. They can cry often, have outbursts, or suddenly disappear from the face of the earth and go underground. These signs are mistaken as mental or emotional weakness, but it is just a way of empaths to vent if they don't get enough solitary time to recuperate.

Empaths think too much

Empaths are often accused of thinking too much and unnecessarily because of their naturally curios nature. Questions about the universe and life give empaths a philosophical personality. They are often at the receiving end of statements like "Where do you find such questions?", "How do you come up with such stuff?", or "Why do you think so much?" The questions that confound empaths are usually heavy topics of discussion for other people, giving them the title of over thinkers.

Empaths and Sensitive People

There is a basic, albeit fine, difference between an empath and a highly sensitive person (HSP). An empath absorbs and feels the emotional and physical states of other people as if they are going through it personally. HSPs are very sensitive to external stimuli and often feel in-tune with their surroundings. They are also prone to high levels of emotion and can get overwhelmed easily. Empaths generally have a highly-developed intuition, whereas HSPs have a sensitive nervous system that makes them so reactive to the outside world.

An estimated 15 to 20% of people in the world are HSPs while only 2 to 3% are empaths. Empaths pick up on the emotions that people project and HSPs pick up on energies that affect their senses.

Again, these two are quite different from the basic trait of empathy that is naturally present in human beings, barring sociopaths and people with mental disorders. All empaths are highly sensitive, but not all HSPs are empaths. The basic difference is that an HSP is only sensitive to the energies and emotions surrounding him/her, whereas an empath can actually feel those emotions as his/her own.

For example, if you are an HSP sitting with a friend who has just been through a bad breakup and is crying, you will feel the energy that she is emanating and it will affect you physically. You will get upset and feel bad for the friend. However, if you are empath, you will be feeling exactly what your friend is feeling – betrayed, anxious, alone, hurt, sad, and lonely. You may feel one or many of these emotions, like it is happening to *you*. Empaths can feel not just the emotions, but also the physical symptoms accompanying them. For example, if your friend gets a headache from crying, or develops a cold, you may develop it too. Or you may also feel a sudden exhaustion and depletion of emotional energy like your friend does.

HSPs have an equally difficult time trying to sort out their emotions from those of the other person as an empath does. However, as they cannot absorb the other person's emotional energies and feel the same things, they often confuse their own feelings for those of the others. Sensitive people cry and feel extremely down in the face of another person's tragedy, but cannot actually feel their pain. If they learn to control their sensitive side though, they can be great support systems owing to their nature. They sometimes fail to understand that what they are projecting outward isn't necessarily the emotional energy of another person, but their own reaction to the same. Once they are able to make the differentiation, they can better utilize their sensitive nature for the good of others.

Empaths on the other hand tend to merge with other people and mix their emotional energies as well. Although they are in their own bodies, their soul may seem to be temporarily intertwined with another. This nature is slightly deeper than 'putting yourself in another's shoes'. They feel the exact same emotions that the other person is projecting, and a part of them becomes that person.

Empaths project emotions on a much lower level than sensitive people. Sensitive people project their emotions outward as a means to cope with the overwhelming energies. Their nature is such that these energies go beyond their capacity to cope, and hence reacting and venting are their best protection mechanisms. On the contrary, empaths absorb the outward projected emotional energies and mix it with their own, thus feeling those exact emotions. Both empaths and HSPs are sensitive to external stimuli and emotions. However, one of them tends to absorb them and the other tends to only feel them.

Most of the time, empaths are misunderstood to be highly sensitive and HSPs are misunderstood as empaths. Sensitive people can make themselves more resilient to external sensory stimuli using techniques like meditation, defining mental and emotional boundaries, and practicing mindfulness and self-awareness. Empaths, on the other hand, need to learn how to harness their gift, control it, and make it stronger.

If you believe that you possess either one of these natures, then read the above-mentioned traits one more time to understand what your nature exactly is. Knowing whether you are an empath or highly sensitive in nature will help you find the best coping mechanisms and methods to better harness it.

Types of Empaths

Once you have figured out whether you are an empath, the next thing to know is what kind of empath you are. Empaths absorb the emotions of others, mixing it with their own. They literally feel what the other person is going through, both emotionally and physically. However, there are differences in what empaths respond the most to. Once you know what kind of empath you are, you can better enhance and control your abilities because it will be easier for you to understand your feelings and help others through it.

Physical Empath

A physical empath can either be physically intuitive or physically one with another, and sometimes even both. Physically intuitive empaths can understand when someone else is having a physical discomfort. Although they cannot feel the physical symptoms, they can feel the emotional unease caused by them. The physical oneness empath will feel the same symptoms as those of the person near them. In this case, you will get a headache or feel nauseous just like the other person. The latter type of empath ability is tricky because the empath won't understand why they are suffering from unexplained aches and pains. Although it will be bothersome initially, honing this gift can allow the empath to help a lot of people.

Emotional Empath

Emotional empaths are also of two types – intuitive and possessing oneness. The former kind of empath knows what a person is feeling despite hearing contradictory words. For example, you will know if your friend is in low spirits even if they say they are fine. These empaths can work around the facades and denial, and get a person to open up. Empaths that possess emotional oneness can actually feel the emotions of another person. So, if your friend is feeling low and depressed, so will you. These empaths absorb the feelings of the other person and mix it with their own. This makes it difficult for them to differentiate their own feelings from the ones they are absorbing, which often leads to mood swings and depression.

Intellectual Empath

Intellectual empaths manage to merge their intellectual wavelength with that of the other person and accordingly alter the way they communicate. Hence, if they are talking to someone who doesn't know English very well, they'll automatically use simpler words, or if someone has a very refined language, then they will use longer words. Intellectual empaths have a very good knack for effective communication. They can alter the way the converse, both verbally and non-verbally, to put the other person at ease and communicate in the most efficient way possible. Intellectual empaths can be great speakers or performers in the fields of their choice because of their natural ability to be convincing in their communication.

Animal Empath

This one isn't very hard to figure out. Animal empaths, or fauna empaths, feel a special connect towards animals. These people can often be found gravitating towards animals and even having long conversations with them. They can understand what an animal is feeling – discomfort, happiness, sadness, and even feel the same emotions or physical conditions. This makes them great at helping animals in many ways. Fauna empaths are excellent vets and animal experts owing to their natural gift. They can help people who have pets, animals in zoos and sanctuaries, and even animals in shelters, as volunteers.

Plant Empath

Plant empaths, also known as flora empaths, have a special connection towards plants. They can understand how it is to be a particular tree or flower or plant. They can feel the emotions of a plant and know whether it is happy or unhappy. Flora empaths usually have beautiful gardens full of flowers, herbs, or vegetables, and can even be really good at cooking with spices. They communicate with plants on a very 'soul' level.

Claircognizant Empath

Remember the empathic trait of 'just knowing' things? These empaths are called claircognizants. They have a strong feeling about things that need to be done or when something is untrue, without any indications towards the same. This often leaves other people wondering how the empath knows these things. Empaths who strengthen these qualities can accurately know when something is wrong, or when something is about to happen. They have highly tuned intuitive and psychic powers.

Geomatic Empath

Geomatic empaths can read the signals that the earth transmits in the form of energy. They can predict if a natural disaster is about to take place because of their ability to catch the energy waves coming from the earth.

Environmental Empath

These empaths can feel the energy in a particular surrounding. If they are among nature, it means more to them than just being around trees. They can feel the energies of the trees, soil, rocks, air, and everything around them. This can make them emotional. They feel like the surroundings are communicating with them.

Medium Empath

Medium empaths can usually feel, see, and/or hear spirits. They are often known as psychic mediums. Medium empaths can communicate with those that are beyond the physical realm and present around us in spirit form; for example, the deceased. They are also known as clairvoyants and make for popular subjects in movie plots, like the Demi Moore-Patrick Swayze starrer *Ghost*. There are many items that have become symbolic of clairvoyants or mediums, like the crystal ball and card reading.

Psychometric Empath

Psychometric empaths feel a connection with inanimate objects. They can connect with an object and feel the energies of any previous owners or any other strong feelings that have attached to it. Sometimes, an object tells them stories of its past too. It is often difficult for psychometric empaths to use/buy/keep items that have been previously owned because of the energies attached to them.

Precognitive Empath

Precognitive empaths are those we can call truly psychic. They can sense an event about to happen before it actually does. Those with greater control over their ability can develop this sense to a greater ability. They can either feel it physically or emotionally, like a niggling feeling that something is about to happen, or it can be manifested in the form of dreams and visions.

Telepathic Empath

Telepathic empaths can read another person's mind, though not quite literally. They have a gift of understanding what another person is thinking despite the words that he/she is saying. These people can sense what the other person is about to say or do and what is going through their mind. They can also sense the intentions of the thoughts; whether they are good or bad. A telepathic empath can often give the other person a feeling of 'being inside their head'.

Controlling and Strengthening your Empathic Abilities

Empaths are naturally gifted people because of their ability to absorb and feel the emotions coming from their surroundings. As it goes for all natural abilities and talents, an empathic personality also needs to be honed and refined. It needs control, strengthening, and practice. Empaths cannot just decide to shut off from the world and become distant because it goes against their nature.

Once you realize that you are an empath, you should start working on using your abilities to their best potential, and there are many ways to do this. Listed below are some techniques and methods to control and strengthen your empathic traits. Let's start from the very basic step of becoming aware and then move on to more concrete methods.

Become Aware of Your Gift

The very first step in controlling and strengthening your empathic abilities is to become aware of the fact that you are an empath. Once you know that, you have to go about understanding how it works, what you can actually do, and how you should separate your own feelings from those that you are picking up from your surroundings.

When you are engulfed by an emotion for no reason, take a pause and look around. Ask yourself whether these feelings are yours or someone else's. Watch your thoughts. You will eventually be able to differentiate between the two in a better way. The same goes for emotional vampires and narcissists, as well as people who bring you down. Once you realize how poisonous they are for you, you will learn to distance and protect yourself.

For people who don't know they are empaths, the period before they understand it is particularly tough. It is emotionally draining and mentally exhausting. From knowing that you are empath to having a strong hold on your abilities takes time, patience, learning, and experiences. It isn't easy, but the lessons are valuable. Once you are aware of this gift that is bestowed upon you, you can do wonderful things with it.

Use Your Gift

Once you understand your ability to absorb the emotions of others and mix them up with your own, you will be able to take steps to keep yourself free of those energies and yet be there for the people around you. To begin with, you need to start figuring out what you need and when you need it. Being considerate and accepting of your ability will help you offer support or help to those who need it. If there is tension or nervousness in the air, then you can offer support instead of taking on the same feeling. If your friend is feeling depressed, then you can be there for her/him and help them get out of it if you are able to strengthen your ability instead of letting it affect you adversely.

There are many techniques that you can use to both control and strengthen your empathic abilities. These range from mental practices to physical activities.

Practice meditation

Meditation is one of the best ways to calm the mind and reduce internal chaos. It also helps you focus better on important things without getting distracted. Most importantly, though, meditation helps to develop intuition.

It communicates with you in the form of visions and messages that you need to decipher for receiving the answers. When you begin meditating for the first time, start off slowly with a few minutes a day. Remember, meditation is a gradual process and takes time to master. It also differs greatly from person to person. However, it is known to be very effective for peace of mind and gaining highly-developed intuition.

Yoga

Yoga is similar to meditation because it calms the mind. It does have many physical benefits, obviously, but it is particularly effective for mental strength. Yoga fortifies and soothes the body. Complicated *asanas* pose as a hurdle that the mind needs to overcome, resulting in a partnership between the mind and the body. Yoga helps in an all-round development of the mind whilst giving the body a good workout. There are a lot of yoga videos and articles available on the internet highlighting its benefits. However, you should consider starting off with an actual class where you will learn the correct techniques and methods from a professional instructor. Once you have the basics covered, consider doing it at home.

Create a Shield

You can use visualization and verbal reinforcement to create a protective shield around you that clearly distinguishes you from the outside world. This will help you to create a proper differentiation between your emotions and those coming from others. Create an imaginary shield around you. Be as specific and vivid as you can so that it's easier to picture it. Keep telling yourself that this shield will protect you from external emotional energies. The shield or force field is made up of energy, and is a creation of your mind. Ask your mind to help you, and be very clear and persistent. If you feel an influx of emotional energies, you can simply think about your shield and imagine it safely surrounding you. That way, you can protect yourself from getting affected from absorbing by the emotions around you and yet understand what the other person is going through.

Activate Your Chakras

There are various chakras located in the human body, and activating or opening them brings about a lot of spiritual and mental benefits. The different chakras are root chakra, sacral chakra, solar plexus chakra, throat chakra, third eye chakra, heart chakra, and crown chakra. There are various techniques to activate the chakras, yoga and meditation being a few of them. Look for live classes and internet tutorials to know how to do it. The chakras help you connect to the earth and your own self on a deep, spiritual level. They help develop intuition and mental strength to better harness your empathic powers. One way to activate your chakras is through yoga. There are many other methods for which you should turn to your *guru*, various books, or to the internet.

Cleanse Your Etheric Body

Empaths tend to be bearers and harbingers of the emotional energies around them. This energy builds up over time, taking up a lot mental and emotional space. If you don't clear this build up regularly, it can take a toll on your mental and physical well-being. This can lead to depression, becoming withdrawn, losing interest in doing things, getting annoyed or irritated, cold or distant, or just feeling like you're losing your mind. It is kind of the same as living in a room that hasn't been cleaned for months, and has clothes, books, shoes, and all other clutter just lying scattered.

Hence, cleaning out all the vibes and emotions from time to time is extremely important. This can be achieved by meditation, visualization of a cleansing light coursing through your body and ridding it of all the clutter, using the power of the mind to clean out the vibes, remaining grounded and connected to the earth, and also using verbal reinforcement. These methods must be used a few times a day for a few days for them to be effective, especially if you are new at it. It is very important to do this as soon as you start to feel burdened or mentally/emotionally 'exhausted'. Dealing with all the built-up vibes is very important.

Chants and Prayers

Chanting, prayers, and verbal reinforcements help strengthen your empathic abilities as well as protect you from external energies. The mind does what you tell it to, and hence, reassuring yourself with verbal stimulation can help reprogram your mind. Chanting releases certain vibrations into the universe, which are made of energies and can be quite powerful. These vibrations can be used to visualize and create that protective force field around yourself, or to ask the universe for the strength to take on the external influences coming your way. You can create your own power-statements or reinforcements for repeating throughout the day. They should be short and precise, easy to remember, and easy to visualize.

The Volume Buttons Technique

This is a very popular technique for building a great defense against external energies that you end up absorbing, so that they don't affect you. The technique goes such that you have to imagine two volume buttons, one that represents your emotions and the other that represents other people's emotions. Now assign a value to each. If you are taking in a lot of external emotions, then the second dial should have a higher value. And if your emotional energy is low and mixed with that of others, then your dial should be low.

Now visualize that you are reducing the value of the second dial, but only slightly. Then visualize your own dial value going up very slightly. This means that you are putting your emotions first and not mixing them with those of others. Conscious and consistent visualization, a number of times a day for as long as you need, will finally help you get your dial up to a 10 and the other one down to a 1 or 2. The key here is to be consistent, maintain realistic goals and patience to reprogram your mind and be less affected by outside energies.

Focus on Your Physical Being

Focus on being present in your own body; let's understand this with an example. Imagine you are at a fair or a club, or any other public place, and start getting overwhelmed by all the emotions that are coming your way and mixing with your own. What do you do? Focus inward. Feel your core. Feel your arms and legs and head. Be conscious of where you are sitting, where your feet are, what you are eating, or where you are standing. Feel the air making contact with your body. Feel your heartbeat. Once you have blocked out everything else and focused on yourself, then go about building your energy force field to help stop emotions from outside affecting you.

Set Limits, Don't Become a Dumping Ground

When dealing with other people, you need to set limits on your level of involvement and how much you allow another person to take advantage of your nature. Taking responsibility for your own emotions is very important. Empaths are easy targets for narcissistic people, emotional vampires, and pessimistic people. Hence, you need to understand where to draw the line and say no. This will not only help you remain grounded and sane, but also allow you to help those who are genuinely looking for some solutions or guidance. Empaths run the risk of becoming emotional dumping grounds for people who just want to vent out their negative emotions without taking any responsibility for them. It takes time for empaths to understand the genuine people from the emotional vampires, but once you have learnt your lesson, you should set limits, be firm, and never repeat the same mistakes again. If you need some verbal reinforcement, then keep telling yourself that it isn't your responsibility to take on someone else's emotions. You do

NOT need to feel sorry about creating a safe and protective distance from people who thrive on emotional reactions and will do anything to provoke you for an emotion. Believe that you are more important and understand that not everyone comes from a good place. Some people are self-centered and use you for their own personal agendas.

Understand Your Mind

When you know yourself in and out, you will be able to separate your emotions from those of others around you much better. Know your mind well. Know what triggers you, what makes you happy, what makes you sad, and what state of mind you are predisposed to. Understand whether you are mostly happy, mostly down, and also how different situations make you feel. Being completely informed about who you are, and how your mind works will help ease your confusion when other emotions start mixing with yours. When you are already aware of your emotions, a sudden change can be categorized as someone else's emotional energy. This will help you stop the feelings right there, separate them from yours, and work on shielding yourself from any more influxes.

Be Aware of Negativity

Negativity, sadness, and suffering are all around us. And for empaths, these situations can be particularly terrifying because they can actually feel the fear, pain, anxiety, betrayal, and all the other feelings that the victim felt. And this can send them into a downward spiral. Although it is impossible to avoid such situations, it is possible to control their impact on you. When you start to feel any of the above-mentioned emotions, try one simple thing. Become hyper aware of your body and your physical state and cut off all external noise as well as any other thoughts that you are having, including the negative ones. Then tell yourself, very clearly and as many times as you have to, that you are not present in that situation nor are you a part of it, and that there is NOTHING that you can do about it. If there is something you can do to help, then being an empath, you are probably already doing it. Otherwise, understand that although it is very unfortunate, bad things happen, and not feeling bad about it does not make you a horrible person. Keep reinforcing the above statement until you feel better.

Take Intuition Development or Meditation Classes

These classes are helpful and necessary for one very primary reason that it is a gathering of like-minded people who understand each other and can offer the correct and right kind of help and guidance. For novice empaths who are under-informed about strengthening their abilities, as well as those who want to increase their intuitive powers, it is always better to start off with a group than going solo. You should look for a class that gives you a 'good feeling'. If it feels right, safe, trustworthy, and non-judgmental, at least to a great degree, then join in. Otherwise, keep looking, because you know what happens if you take up an activity where the surroundings make you uncomfortable.

Keep a Meditation Diary

Keep a meditation diary for all your meditation experiences. After every meditation session, note down all the visions that you had and any messages you thought you received. Even if you don't write your perception of every vision, just write about what you saw. Sometimes, these messages are not meant to be understood by us until the time is right, which can be after days, weeks, months, or even years. These visions will help in your aim of strengthening your intuitive powers. Keeping a diary is important because you will soon forget what you saw, and then the message will be lost.

Note Down Your Intuitions

You can have a separate book for this or just use your meditation diary. Make a note of whatever gut feeling you had throughout the day, and what the outcome of these feelings was. You should be as elaborate as you can, listing down your entire thought process, perceptions, and reasons.

Analyze it as much as you want, and delve deeper into it. Keep doing this on a daily basis. You can go back to these experiences in the future and borrow from them for any lessons, like where you went wrong and what you thought should have been done at that time. This is where being elaborate and descriptive will help, because we don't remember things that happened in the past and what our exact thoughts were at the time; at least not accurately.

Go Online

As a last resort, or a first one, check the internet for more or basic information on how to go about handling your empathic nature. There are hundreds of articles online that will guide you on the traits of empaths and how to know if you are one. You will also find numerous tutorials, readings, virtual classrooms, and articles on harnessing, controlling, and strengthening your empathic abilities. However, remember that articles and most of the resources only serve as a guide, and to actually understand and learn the processes may take some expert help. Interacting with like-minded people and maybe joining some groups can be a lot more helpful in the beginning so that you don't learn the wrong things. Misinformed or half-informed actions are never effective. Hence, remember that you are not alone and help and guidance are always available should you seek them.

Understand How Your Emotions Participate

Empaths and emotions are very closely connected, which is why it is important for empaths to be in control of their own emotions whilst not being drained out by those of others. Here are some very important things about emotions that you need to remember as an empath so that it doesn't affect you in an adverse way, positively or negatively.

1. Emotions influence and control your thoughts. It is very easy to be overcome by emotions and react instead of responding rationally. You must have heard

the phrase 'thinking with your heart'? It means that when our emotions take over, the mind takes a backseat and our responses turn into impulsive emotion-driven reactions. This can happen to empaths more often than other people, and understandably, you need to remember this.

2. Emotions also influence your physical responses. Being present in a situation where another person has suffered physical harm can make an empath feel the same pain and discomfort. In this case, your physical responses will only cause you pain, and you won't be able to help in the situation even if you want to. Practice grounding and verbal reinforcements to distance yourself from external emotions so that your emotions don't get mixed up and you can act objectively.

3.   It is possible to control your emotional responses. It sometimes seems like emotions come out of nowhere and are impossible to control. However, that is far from the case. Other than the instinctive fight and flight responses, other reactions can be controlled. What it needs is a high level of awareness and practice. Taking a step back, calming down, and looking at the situation objectively are the best way to have a handle on your emotional outbursts. It takes time, so start practicing.

4.   One very important way to keep yourself light and happy is to not be in denial of your feelings, acknowledge them, and actually feel them. If you don't feel your emotions and vent them, it will keep building up in your mind and lead to depression, introvert behavior, anxiety, and irritation among

other things. It is scary to face your emotions and issues, but it needs to be done for the sake of your sanity. Get to the root of your emotions, find the cause, and deal with it in your way. This will help you be more at peace with yourself.

5. It is very easy to set our thoughts and reactions on auto pilot and jump to a known response before assessing the entire situation. Empaths can especially get carried away and react to an external stimulus without taking some time to think about it rationally. This can have an effect on your mental well-being.

6. Try not to get infected by the moods of others. Even if one person reacts in a certain way, it can cause a shift in your mood if it is someone that you are very close to. It is easy to get caught up. Remember the

techniques we talked about above and create a distance.

Remember that being emotionally empathetic isn't always helpful or good. It can lead to you becoming a dumping ground for emotional vampires. These are people who know how to instigate emotional reactions out of you. Learn to gauge whether a person is genuine or not. Time will definitely tell. Once you understand this, it will be easier to create a healthy distance.

In Conclusion

Did you know that great leaders and personalities like Mahatma Gandhi and Mother Teresa were believed to be empathic? They did a lot of commendable work for the good of other people, whilst keeping their own needs aside. To do such selfless work for the benefit of others requires some real mental, emotional, and spiritual power.

Empaths are also popular in fictional movies and books. For example, Superwoman, Yoda and Aqua man are well-known fictional characters that were believed to be empaths. More recently, the characters of Alice and Edward Cullen from the *Twilight* series can be said to possess certain empathic qualities like predicting the future and hearing other's thoughts. Although these have a more magical depiction, the 'gifts' are very close to empathic qualities.

Being an empath is nothing short of amazing, because of how rare your gift is. Less than 10% of the world is believed to possess what you have, so that makes you pretty unique doesn't it? Imagine what you can achieve if you harness this gift and strengthen it. You can help other beings and make a difference, however small.

It is very important to understand your abilities and accept them in order to hone them further. It takes time, patience, practice, some amount of frustration, and a lot of learned lessons along the way. Once you get there though, it is absolutely worth it. Being able to understand what another living being is feeling or trying to communicate, naturally, is nothing short of amazing. It can be of immense help to those who need it.

You are an Empath, and you can make a difference.

I want to thank you from the bottom of my heart for taking the time to read this book! I hope that this book has brought you much understanding and has provided some value to you and your empathic abilities. If you enjoyed this book please leave a 5-star review on amazon telling me what you liked best about the book. Thanks so much, and have a great day!

-Jason Bennett

Made in the USA
San Bernardino, CA
06 February 2018